Baby Animals in the Wild!

Fox Kits in the Wild

by Katie Chanez

Bullfrog Books

Ideas for Parents and Teachers

Bullfrog Books let children practice reading informational text at the earliest reading levels. Repetition, familiar words, and photo labels support early readers.

Before Reading

- Discuss the cover photo. What does it tell them?

- Look at the picture glossary together. Read and discuss the words.

Read the Book

- "Walk" through the book and look at the photos. Let the child ask questions. Point out the photo labels.

- Read the book to the child, or have him or her read independently.

After Reading

- Prompt the child to think more. Ask: Fox kits learn from their mom. What does their mom teach them to do?

Bullfrog Books are published by Jump!
5357 Penn Avenue South
Minneapolis, MN 55419
www.jumplibrary.com

Copyright © 2024 Jump! International copyright reserved in all countries. No part of this book may be reproduced in any form without written permission from the publisher.

Library of Congress Cataloging-in-Publication Data

Names: Chanez, Katie, author.
Title: Fox kits in the wild / by Katie Chanez.
Description: Minneapolis, MN: Jump!, Inc., [2024]
Series: Baby animals in the wild! | Includes index.
Audience: Ages 5–8
Identifiers: LCCN 2022043032 (print)
LCCN 2022043033 (ebook)
ISBN 9798885244060 (hardcover)
ISBN 9798885244077 (paperback)
ISBN 9798885244084 (ebook)
Subjects: LCSH: Foxes—Infancy—Juvenile literature.
Classification: LCC QL737.C22 C413 2024 (print)
LCC QL737.C22 (ebook)
DDC 599.77513/92—dc23/eng/20221223
LC record available at https://lccn.loc.gov/2022043032
LC ebook record available at https://lccn.loc.gov/2022043033

Editor: Eliza Leahy
Designer: Molly Ballanger

Photo Credits: Richard Seeley/Shutterstock, cover; Eric Isselee/Shutterstock, 1, 3, 22, 24; blickwinkel/Alamy, 4, 23bm; Miroslav Hlavko/Shutterstock, 5, 23tm; Cyril Ruoso/Nature Picture Library/SuperStock, 6–7, 23bl; Geoffrey Kuchera/Shutterstock, 8–9, 23tl; pchoui/iStock, 10; SERGEI BRIK/Shutterstock, 11; Carlos Carreno/Getty, 12–13; AngelaLouwe/Shutterstock, 14–15, 23br; Menno Schaefer/Shutterstock, 16; David Kalosson/Shutterstock, 17; Freder/iStock, 18–19, 23tr; Albert Beukhof/Shutterstock, 20–21.

Printed in the United States of America at Corporate Graphics in North Mankato, Minnesota.

Table of Contents

Part of the Litter 4
Parts of a Fox Kit 22
Picture Glossary 23
Index 24
To Learn More 24

Part of the Litter

These babies are new. They are fox kits!

kit

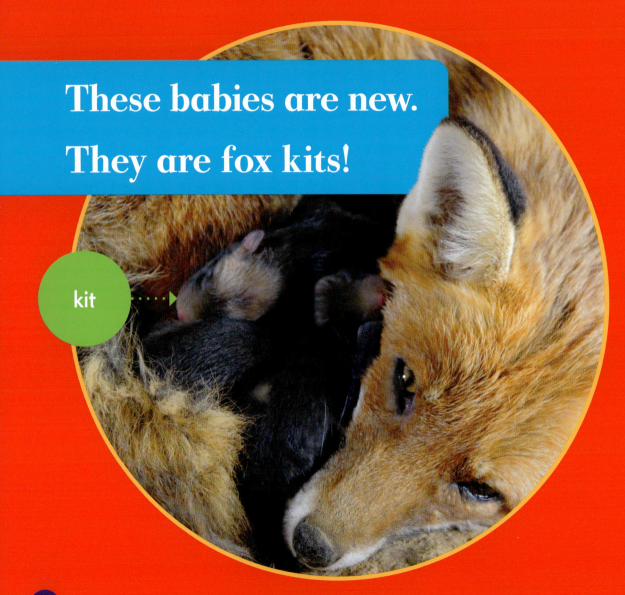

They are born in a den.

There are several in the litter.

litter

Fur keeps them warm.
It is gray or brown.
It turns red as they grow.

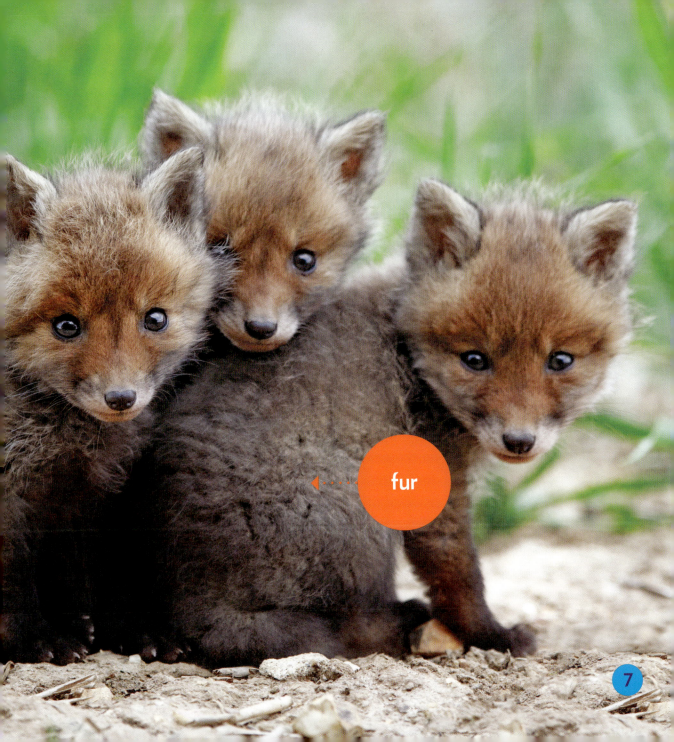

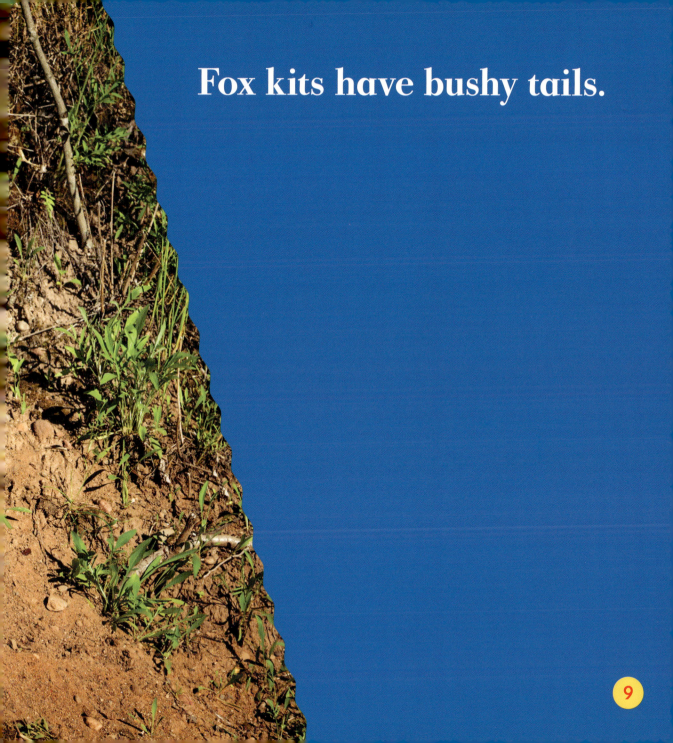

Fox kits have bushy tails.

The kits drink Mom's milk.

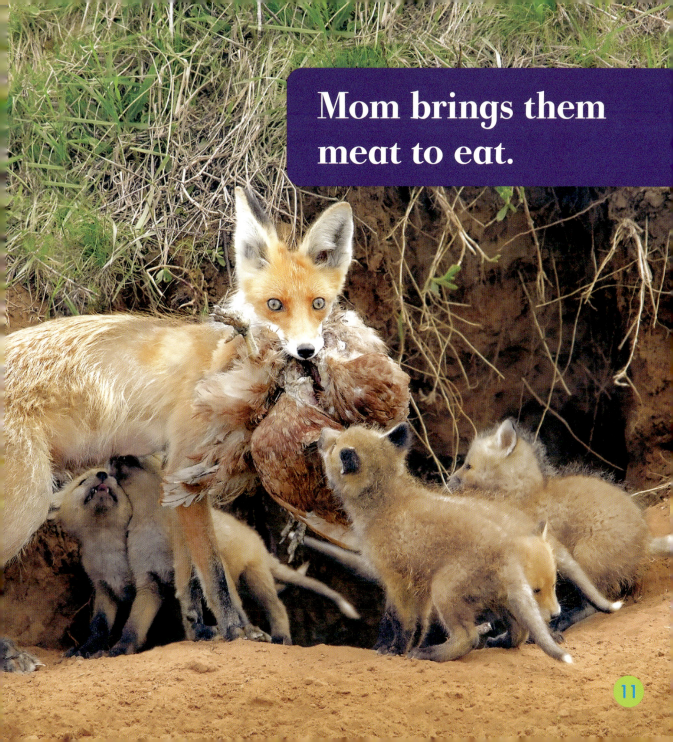

Mom brings them meat to eat.

The kits grow.
They run!

They join a group.
It is called a skulk.

They learn to hunt.
How?
They play.

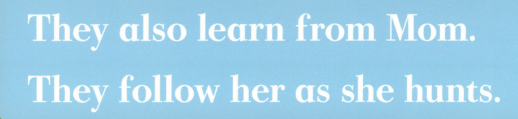

They also learn from Mom.
They follow her as she hunts.

This kit hunts alone.
It catches a bird.
Yum!

19

It grows up.
It has kits of its own!

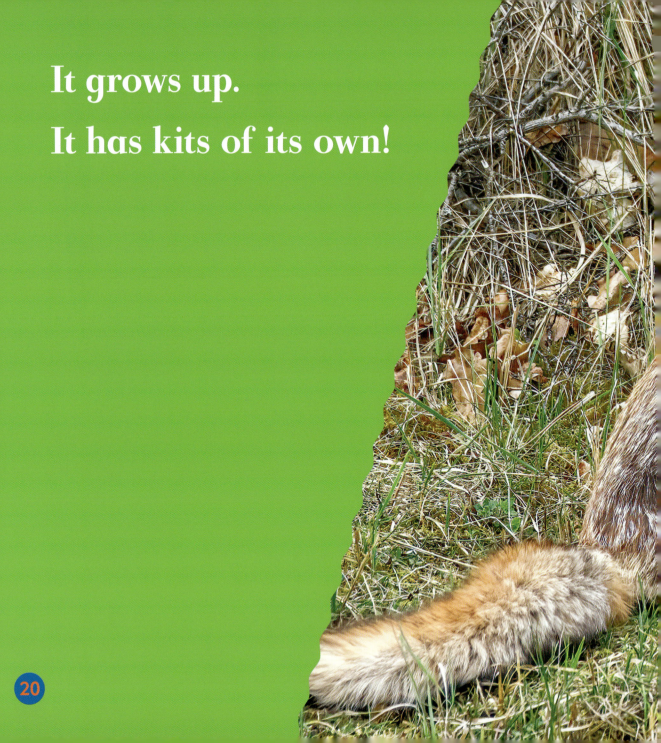

Parts of a Fox Kit

What are the parts of a fox kit? Take a look!

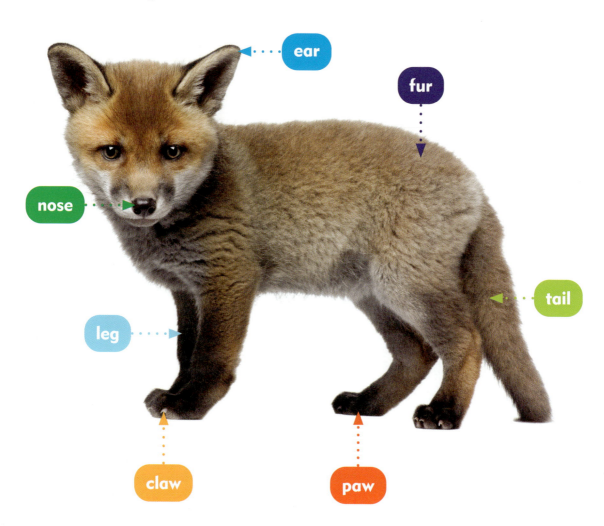

Picture Glossary

bushy
Thick and fluffy.

den
The home of a wild animal.

hunt
To chase and kill animals for food.

kits
Baby foxes.

litter
A number of fox kits that are born at the same time to the same mother.

skulk
A group of foxes.

Index

den 5
fur 6
grow 6, 13, 20
hunt 16, 17, 19
litter 5
meat 11
milk 10
Mom 10, 11, 17
play 16
run 13
skulk 14
tails 9

To Learn More

Finding more information is as easy as 1, 2, 3.

❶ Go to www.factsurfer.com

❷ Enter "foxkits" into the search box.

❸ Choose your book to see a list of websites.